HOW TO GROW YOUR BUSINESS WITH VOICE SEARCH

7 STEPS TO RANK YOUR BUSINESS BY VOICE SEARCH

JESSICA ZEITZ
MANDI GOULD
ALLAN MUNRO

"The Only Thing That Is Constant Is Change"

Heraclitus

Contents

Preface

I have always been an early adopter and enjoyed working on projects that had no rules, no boundaries, and the only instruction was 'figure out how to do 'X,' then do it.

In the past few years, I have been involved in startups, the growth of the online business world, and have been spending time at the intersection of experienced business people and where they meet and work with the younger generation of millennials, where all technology is not a technology to them. Instead, it just is what it is.

I have discovered in this space between these two generations, the ones with the business wisdom working with alongside the younger generation that knows how to do things, that there is a gray area that needs some explaining, and it is here where the mystery can is explained.

The new opportunities in Voice Search are one of these areas that need some explaining and some formal clarification. In working with Mandi Gould and her team at Barker Social in the past, I thought we could unshroud some of the mystery in Voice Search and how Voice Search works, what it is based on, how it is different from traditional search, and most importantly, how you can get your business and website ready for the growth of Voice Search and the waves of change we will see in its wake.

Thanks for reading.

Allan Munro
Toronto, Canada.
May 2019

Acknowledgements

I would like to thank Mandi Gould for assembling her team to mobilize the work done on this project. Mandi's commitment and unbelievable stick-to-itiveness is amazing. Jessica Zeitz for her clarity in words, and the research and SEO expertise of Pablo Zambrano who relentlessly clarified all the things we needed to verify.

Introduction

Optimizing your Website: SEO for Voice Search

The next serious disruption to digital marketing has arrived... and almost no one is ready for it.

Siri, Alexa, and Google assistant are only the beginning. What may have begun as asking Siri for the weather forecast, Google for directions, or Alexa to play your favorite song is quickly changing the way that businesses operate on the internet forever. The implications of Voice Search are massive and it's only a matter of time before the majority of online searches become hands-free.

Is your business ready for it?

Part 1
Getting Up to Speed

- Overview
- The Explosive Growth of Voice Search
- Internet Search Versus Home Assistant
- Market Data
- How Voice Search is Getting Smarter
- Front End and Back End of Search

Overview

What is Voice Search?

Voice Search is speech recognition technology that allows users to search by speaking out loud instead of typing search terms into a search bar either on a mobile phone, tablet, personal computer, or smart car interface. What had started out as a novelty is now changing the way a user interacts with websites and apps and is quickly revolutionizing how users are searching for information and services.

If you are trying to find a restaurant on your phone or computer, chances are you will type something like, "best restaurants New York City" — this is computer language.

Whereas, if you use voice search, you will probably say something like:

"Hey Google, what's the best restaurant near me that's serving dinner right now?"

That is voice search language, which is more likely to contain question phrases or natural queries.

So, why is this important? Since voice behavior is different from traditional browser search behavior, Google ranks voice search differently.

Yes, that's right. Google is treating voice searches differently than typed searches and your regular SEO rankings may not transfer to your Voice Search rankings.

So, if you want to be on top of your business' SEO it's vital that you aren't neglecting Voice Search when creating and optimizing your content. That means you need to be thinking about Voice SEO, aka. Voice Search Engine Optimization, aka. optimizing your website so that the voice assistant tools will be able to find you.

The Explosive Growth of
Voice Search

It is NOT a Fad

Voice search has moved well beyond tech-savvy early adopters and has gained mileage in the mainstream market. This momentum is only going to build in the coming 2-3 years as convenience overtakes questions about the still-new technology.

If you don't believe voice search is here to stay check out these trends and usage data.

- Amazon has 7000 employees reviewing Alexa Voice Requests, each reviewing up to 1000 searches a day. Consider that for a moment: Amazon is reviewing up to **7,000,000** Voice Searches a day that Alexa can not understand.[1]

- Voice labs discovered a total of <u>33 million voice-first devices</u> in circulation.[2]

- In a survey of <u>SEO trends for 2017 and beyond</u>, voice search earned the *third* spot. And now it's 2019, so that number has certainly increased.[3]

- Google CEO Sundar Pichai revealed in a keynote speech that one-fifth of Google queries are Voice Searches.[4]

---

1 Bloomberg News April 10, 2019 Technology Amazon Workers Are Listening to What You Tell Alexa

2 https://searchengineland.com/30-million-voice-first-devices-us-homes-year-end-report-268003

3 Aaron Wall, SEO Expert July 6, 2016 https://alamedaim.com/seo-trends/

4 Greg Sterling on May 18, 2016 serachengineland.com https://searchengineland.com/google-reveals-20-percent-queries-voice-queries-249917

- <u>Technavio</u> found that the Voice Recognition Market will reach $601 million by the end of 2019.[5]
- And <u>Alpine.AI</u> found that as of January 2018, there were an estimated one billion voice searches every single month.[6]

These are some serious numbers and unless you want to let your business go the way of the Dodo, you can't ignore the impact that this will have on your business. Your potential customers are certainly moving toward Voice Search!

5https://www.technavio.com/report/global-voice-recognition-biometrics-market-2015-2019?y

6 https://www.wordstream.com/blog/ws/2018/04/10/voice-search-statistics-2018

Internet Search vs. Home Assistant

The Forms of Voice Search

As Voice Search is still in its early development phases and has not fully matured, it is important to distinguish between the two types of Voice Search devices: Mobile Devices versus Home Assistants.

Voice Search on Mobile

For the purposes of this study, we are focusing on Voice Search for mobile devices that have a screen, but this can also include tablets, personal computers, and some Internet Connected Cars. All of these devices have one thing in common; they have a screen for visual display for referencing users search requests.

Home Assistant Devices

Home Assistant Devices are devices used in the home that do not have a screen. Their capabilities can go beyond telling the time, providing the weather report, setting alarms, and listening to music. These Home Assistant Devices are always on and actively listen to everything and are listening for their activation keyword with a search or request from a user.

These devices are rapidly evolving and constantly changing. They include Google Echo, Amazon's Alexa, and Apple's Siri.

As users and companies develop behavior patterns and companies analyze their usage and determine how consumers are interacting with the devices, companies will create business cases to provide services and partner with actual service providers to deliver tangible goods.

Our focus in this guide is to provide businesses with the ability to have their services found by Voice Search, which as of this moment is primarily used on mobile devices and is supported by search engines for the results they generate.

Market Data

Mobile Personal Assistant Use

Voice Search is establishing itself as the wave of the future. Millennials and even more so the upcoming Generation Z are the most at ease using Voice Search with 71% using it on their devices. Teenagers are savvy users of voice search, but Thrive Analytics found that people in all age groups use mobile personal assistants.7 The adoption rate beyond the 40-year-old adult is also strong, which indicates the ease of use of the technology and that users are receiving a benefit from the technology.

Figure 1: Personal Assistant Usage

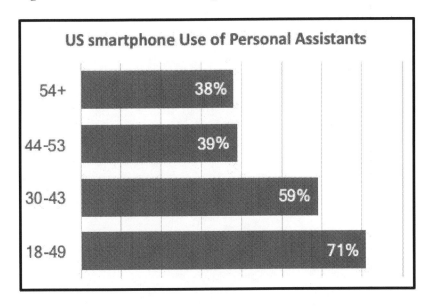

---

7 https://neilpatel.com/blog/seo-for-voice-search/

How Users are Searching for Information

Voice Search is an incredibly powerful tool for brands. 52% of voice-activated speaker owners would like to receive information about deals, sales, and promotions from brands, according to Google. 39% would like to receive options to find business information.8

Figure 2: How Users Search for Information

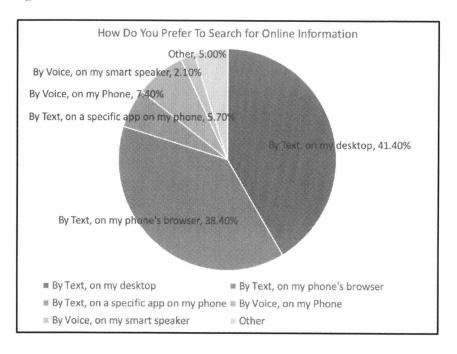

8 January 2018 Think With Google Sara Kleinberg

How Voice Search is Getting Smart
and *So* is Google

At first, Voice Search was slow and clunky often resulting in <u>hilarious mistakes</u> like typing out the words "exclamation mark" or resulting in pure gibberish. But now, voice-operated technology is getting smart… and *fast*.

Artificial intelligence powers Voice Search Engines, and your AI is becoming savvier with every conversation. Today, searches can take into account what has been asked before so you can ask additional questions to narrow down your results. For example, you can ask a Voice Assistant to find all the movies in which Morgan Freeman has appeared. Then, you can narrow it down to ask which Morgan Freeman movies have been Oscar nominated.

Voice Search is also taking context into account. Voice Search Assistants are looking at the world around you to provide more accurate and relevant results. For example, if you're at home you might get different Voice Search results than if you're on your way to work. Or if you're running a specific app, a Voice Search Assistant might use that information to make an educated guess about what you're doing or trying to do. And this will only become more and more intuitive and sophisticated as time goes on.

This ties in directly with user experience, something that Google makes a number one priority. In 2013, Google introduced a major algorithmic update called the <u>Google Hummingbird.</u> The algorithm places greater emphasis on user intent and the contextual meaning of queries, so the user becomes the most important factor when Google creates rankings. Context has become more important than individual keywords. As part of this update, **Google now directs you to the most relevant page on a website, not necessarily to the homepage.**

This means businesses have had to move from stuffing articles full of keywords to actually addressing their target market's pain points with content that offers real value and relevance. Previously, it was common to stuff individual keywords throughout a website or even at the bottom of the website. Now, the context and relevance of the keywords within sentences and the entire body of text takes priority.

Voice technology is just another step in the direction of improving user experience using semantics. Google depends on Natural Language Processing (NLP) to recognize voice texture, interests, and behavior. Over time, Google "learns" your language, accent, and patterns in the way you talk. Then, it focuses on the semantics and the broader contextual relevance of your query to provide a pertinent and seamless user experience.

The Front End and Back End of Search

The market is full of IOT devices; nonstandard computing devices that connect wirelessly to a network and have the ability to transmit data. These include smartphones, tablets, laptops, Voice Assistant devices, and even smart cars. IOT devices can be found in almost every home. The front ends of these devices and the assistants running them are all different and each is competing to be the best with varying degrees of success.

The manufacturer of each IOT device and in particular each Voice Assistant is able to influence which content and partners they allow the consumer to receive results from. They act as a kind of information gatekeeper.

Amazon's Alexa will search its own Amazon database before it goes out to the web for information. Apple's Siri does the same thing. Google will go to its search engine first. It's at this first gate that partnerships and collaborations between businesses will take place.

The backend for virtually all search online is still Google. Google dominates 92% of the search market worldwide.9 In the US, Google represents 89% of search10, and in the EU11 and Canada Google covers 92% of all search.12

China is a closed market to Google, where Baidu covers 71% of the mobile search market, while Google holds just 0.3%.

---

9 http://gs.statcounter.com/search-engine-market-share

10http://gs.statcounter.com/search-engine-market-share/all/united-states-of-america

11 http://gs.statcounter.com/search-engine-market-share/all/europe

12 http://gs.statcounter.com/search-engine-market-share/all/canada

In the western world, regardless of the smartphone device, whether it's Apple, Samsung, or Google, the mobile phones all go back to Google for internet search. However, Amazon's Alexa uses Bing! as its backend search engine after it queries the Amazon databases13. In North America Bing! has a little over 6% of the market share on search14 and is not as 'robust' as the competition.

For almost all businesses, if you want your website to be found by Voice Search, focus on Google first.

---

13 https://thenextweb.com/plugged/2015/07/08/alexa-y-u-no-answer/

14http://gs.statcounter.com/search-engine-market-share/all/united-states-of-america

Part 2

7 Steps to Rank Your Business By Voice Search

Step 1 Copywriting for Voice Search
Step 2 Focus on Conversational Queries
Step 3 Google Map Citations
Step 4 How to Update your 'Google My Business' Profile
Step 5 Optimize for Local Searches
Step 6 Search Result Snippet and Meta Tags
Step 7 Security Matters – SSL Certificates

Step 1

Copywriting for Voice Search

Update Your Content

Voice Search is not only changing the way people search, it's also influencing search engines themselves. That is why you need to closely examine the way you're creating your content.

A. Your keywords should be prominently visible:

- Article headline and page title
- URL slug
- The first paragraph of the article
- Article subheadings

It's critical that you're very clear about the keywords related to your business. Those keywords should be clearly included in all of your content, and carefully placed in headlines, page titles, url slugs, opening paragraphs, and subheadings.

B. Copywriting Should Be Value-Driven

Everything you write should be about your customer, not about you. What benefits are you offering them? What are their needs, problems, desires? Why are they visiting your website in the first place? When you hold your customers' objectives in mind and write with the intent of the reader value, you'll not only hold their attention longer once they arrive on your website, but you'll also help ensure that they find your website in the first place. By providing relevant, client-driven content that is rich in value to your customers, Google will rank you higher in their Voice Search.

C. Write as If You Are Having a Conversation

Keywords are critical to SEO. In the early days of search engine optimization, keyword stuffing was common, but it's no longer a helpful SEO strategy. Instead, you should use natural language and long-tail keywords in your copywriting. When your posts answer questions in an easy to read way, your content will be seen as valuable, and it will rank higher on Google. Instead of keyword stuffing think keyword prominence.

When you sit down to write your copy, picture speaking the words out loud, this will help you produce content with a more conversational flow. Consider the following:

- What questions does my content answer?

- Does my content align with the questions people are asking?

- Does my content provide an all-encompassing, easy to digest answer or is the answer incomplete and not satisfying my customers' needs?

D. Blog Posts

Blog posts are excellent contributors to your overall content and can really enhance the way your website is ranked by Google. Here are some examples of blog posts you can adapt to suit your business that will help answer common questions your target customers might be asking.

Adapt these ideas to suit your business and industry.

- Why XbrandX Washing Machine is the Most Reliable and Cleans Clothing the Best
- Why XbrandX is the Best to Set Up Home Security Camera
- How XbusinessnameX Provides the Best Accounting Services in XlocationX
- What to Look for in a Real Estate Agent in XlocationX
- So, you're looking for the best plumber in XlocationX? Here's what to look for...

You know your business. Pick an angle that has both a problem and a solution. Ask the kinds of questions your customers might ask directly in your blog post to engage your reader while also coming up in Google searches. Make it easy for them to relate the problem to their own situation. Make it feel personal and keep the language simple and easy to read.

TIP

Voice Search-friendly copywriting aligns with the way a user speaks daily and favors natural speech. That means you should use commonly spoken words like 'use' instead of 'utilize' and 'best' instead of 'superior'.

Once you've established the problem, explain the solution. That's where you can give your business a plug in a natural way that isn't overbearingly salesy. By providing helpful content to your reader first before introducing your pitch, you start to win the customer's trust, which results in higher conversion rates.

Do you find it hard to sit down and write? Not everyone is a natural writer, but everyone improves with practice. Here are a few DIY copywriting tips.

Copywriting Process:

A. Give yourself a time limit to write the first draft of each blog post. Create a document (or grab a pencil and paper) and let the ideas flow. We suggest 30 minutes to an hour maximum.

B. Start with an idea that includes a problem and a solution.

C. Jot down the main points that you want the blog post to cover.

D. Ask a question that you can pose to the reader to make the problem relatable to them on a personal level.

E. Explain the problem.

F. Explain the solution.

G. Finish the first draft. Then, set it aside for a day (or more).

H. Return to your first draft later for a second round of tweaks.

I. Always give your second draft to someone else to proofread.

J. Post the article to your blog and make sure to update the snippets and tags. (See section about snippets.)

Tip:
-Don't get caught up in the individual words and sentences in your first draft. You can clean it up later.
-Write to the reader using "you" and "your" so that you're speaking directly to them, not vague to someone else.
-Don't overthink it. Just start writing. You can fix it later. Just get it out of your head.
-If you have another idea for a blog post while you're working on this one, write it down somewhere else (separate document or a post-it note) and save it for later.
-Finish one thing before you start another!

Step 2

Focus on Conversational Queries

Use Natural Language

A. Use 'Long-tail Keywords'

B. Use Question and Answer Approach

C. Featured Snippets

D. Include an FAQ on your website

Your content should use natural language and answer questions people use to make voice search enquiries. Take readability into account, which also reflects on natural spoken language. Reading on the internet is not the same as reading a textbook and neither is the spoken word. You want to make it easy and comfortable for your audience to take in what you have to say. Be straightforward and don't try to sound fancy just for the sake of asserting your professionalism. (Of course, you want to sound like an expert in your market, but if your target market isn't made up of brain surgeons or astrophysics majors, complicated language and long sentences aren't a good idea.)

You'll want to make sure your content is easy to understand, easy to skim, and instantly comprehensible. If you have a WordPress website, the Yoast plugin will help to analyze the readability of your content and Grammarly can also help you improve your writing.

A. Use 'Long-tail Keywords'

Voice Search queries are often more specific than typed questions. So, if you want Google to love your Voice Search optimized content and rank it on the number one page, make sure your content follows a question-answer approach that includes a variety of long-tail keywords.

Long-tail keywords are sets of 3 or more words that go together that are very specific both to what you're selling and to what people are searching for. Here are some examples:

- Game of Thrones all seasons short recap
- Best BBQ restaurant Toronto 2019
- Retro handbags women 1950s pink
- Men's all-star converse high tops white
- Most powerful vacuum under $300 for pets
- Natural eczema cream that really works

Look at the conversational queries people are using. Use Google's autocomplete feature to see what predictions Google will make when you start to type in a question. Google fills in its best predictions of the query to try to figure out what you were probably going to type; it does so by mining real searches that are already popular. Then they show common and trending searches relevant to the words you entered, which are also related to your location and previous searches.

> **Tip**
> *Don't just look over your own data but also verify how your competitors are doing and how they are trying to answer the most relevant questions.*

Wherever you find a Google search box you'll find the autocomplete feature. Whether it's on the Google homepage, in the Google app for iOS and Android, in the quick search box from within Android, or in the "Omnibox" address bar within Chrome, autocomplete finishes your search queries using predictions, so you don't have to type out all the words.

Example: Typing 'york' into Google.

Figure 3: Typing 'york' Into Google

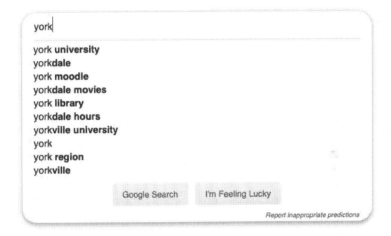

Sometimes, Google's autocomplete feature also helps you finish individual words and phrases, as you type:

Figure 4: Google Autocomplete

best restaurant in new

best restaurant in new **york**
best restaurant in new **york city**
best restaurant in new **orleans**
best restaurant in new **liskeard**
best restaurant in new **delhi**
best restaurant in new **brunswick canada**
best restaurant in new **brunswick**
best restaurant in new **zealand**
best restaurant in new **orleans 2019**
best restaurant in **newmarket**

Google Search   I'm Feeling Lucky

Report inappropriate predictions

B. Use a Question and Answer Approach

Focusing on questions and answers turns your content into a direct solution for a specific problem that someone would vocalize. The more you can hone in on the long-tail keywords for those queries, the higher you will rank by Voice Search.

Think about the question that a user would ask Alexa or Siri and use that as your title. For example, people might ask:

- "How can I optimize my writing for Voice Search?
- "What are the latest Google Home-enabled devices?"
- "What restaurants are open late in Toronto near me?"
- "What's happening in Vancouver this weekend?"

Voice Search-friendly titles would follow the same format:

- "How to Optimize Your Copywriting for Voice Search"
- "What are the latest Google Home-enabled devices for 2019?"
- "What restaurants are open late in Toronto near the Danforth"
- "What's happening in Vancouver April 20-22, 2019"

Keep this approach in mind even for your subheadings and make sure your post directly answers the question being asked.

Answer Who, What, Where, Why, and How questions. Here are some examples:

- Who is the best copywriter in Toronto?
- What do I need for a BBQ?
- Where can I get the best pizza in the Bronx?
- When does the gym open?
- Why do birds suddenly appear?
- How did Google start?

Keep in mind, when your content is fully optimized, Google figures out the question and the answer right from your content. To help optimize your content, try to use short answers and whenever possible present them with bullet points. If you use ten or more steps, Google will add a 'read more' link to the answer box, which can improve your CTR (click-through rate). By using this method to answer questions, your content will not only be ready for Voice Search, but it can also lead to featured snippets on Google.

C. Featured Snippets

What is a featured snippet?15

A Featured Snippet is a clear answer to a question asked in Google. For popular questions with clear answers, Google picks the best answer from the internet and presents it at the top of the search results in its own box. For example, go to Google and type in: "How to write a resume"

There will be a few ads and then you will see something like this, the featured snippet:

Figure 5 Snippet

1. Choose the Right **Resume** Format.
2. Add Your Contact Information and Personal Details.
3. Start with a Heading Statement (**Resume** Summary or **Resume** Objective)
4. List Your Relevant Work Experience & Key Achievements.
5. List Your Education Correctly.
6. Put Relevant Skills that Fit the Job Ad.
7. Include Additional Important **Resume** Sections.

   More items...

How to Make a Resume for a Job [from Application to Interview in 24h]
https://zety.com/blog/how-to-make-a-resume

About this result   Feedback

Notice it was taken from a websites' blog, there is a hyperlink to the blog, and Google shows an image of their webpage.

---

15 https://support.google.com/webmasters/answer/6229325?hl=en

Question and Answer Example:

Sometimes it can be helpful to think of these questions and answers like a recipe. Here's a great example:

How to make the perfect hard-boiled egg (Question)

1. Place your eggs in a single layer on the bottom of your pot and cover with cold water. The water should be about an inch or so higher than the eggs. Cover the pot with a lid.
2. Over high heat, bring your eggs to a rolling boil.
3. Remove from heat and let stand in water for 12 minutes for large eggs. Reduce the time slightly for smaller eggs, and increase the standing time for extra-large eggs.
4. Etc. (read more)

D. Include an FAQ on your website

Another great way to answer questions people are asking is by adding an FAQ page to your website or optimizing the FAQ you already have. It's a great opportunity to clarify questions and answers and to focus on long-tail keywords. It's the perfect opportunity to provide questions and answers so don't miss this chance to win in the search rankings.

Tip

1. Generate your list of Questions

Gather all the questions your customers tend to ask and write a short but relevant answer for each. Search engines can use these answers directly to give searchers an appropriate response for their Voice Search commands.

2. Use Autocomplete to refine your questions

Autocomplete not only makes it easier to complete searches on mobile devices with small screens but it's also a massive time saver. In fact, it reduces typing by approximately 25% on average which cumulatively saves more than 200 years of typing time per day. That's right, per day!16

3. Include 'Long-tail keywords' in your answers.

Most importantly, autocomplete shows you the long-tail keywords that your target customers are actively using on Google. By using these predictions to create questions to answer on your website, you'll ensure that your website comes up first.

---

16   https://www.blog.google/products/search/how-google-autocomplete-works-search/

Step 3

Google Maps Citations

Make Sure Your Data is Accurate

A Google Map citation is when the name of your business is mentioned on another website. For instance, a citation could occur in a business directory like Yelp, Foursquare, or Yahoo Local when your company is mentioned by name. The local citations inherently include a link to your website. When your business information is up to date, you have a better chance of being cited in this way, which is beneficial for your Voice Search rankings.

Figure 6 Google Map Citation

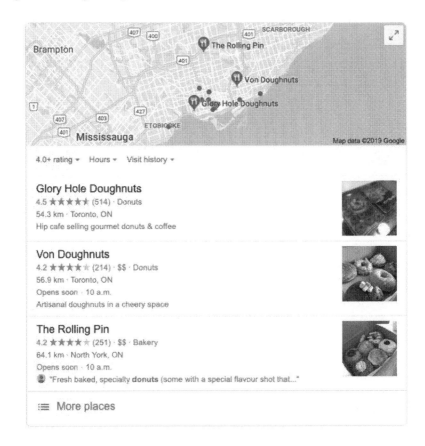

Glory Hole Doughnuts
4.5 ★★★★★ (514) · Donuts
54.3 km · Toronto, ON
Hip cafe selling gourmet donuts & coffee

Von Doughnuts
4.2 ★★★★☆ (214) · $$ · Donuts
56.9 km · Toronto, ON
Opens soon · 10 a.m.
Artisanal doughnuts in a cheery space

The Rolling Pin
4.2 ★★★★☆ (251) · $$ · Bakery
64.1 km · North York, ON
Opens soon · 10 a.m.
🍩 "Fresh baked, specialty donuts (some with a special flavour shot that..."

≡ More places

Always include your business address and phone number so your citation is comprehensive and accurate.

To make sure your map listing ranks high in local map searches, it's imperative that your business name, phone number, and address are consistent in all business directories and citations. Ex: mentions of your name, address, and phone number are always the same.

Citations allow Google to find reputable sources of information about your business to help rank your Google Local map listing. Using map citations, Google can validate your business' existence and legitimacy as well as the accuracy of what you've said about your business by corroborating information about your business from multiple sources.

How Does it Work?

By finding relevant information about your business on other websites, Google can be more confident about the information that you've given them concerning your company. This helps make sure that Google displays your business listing when someone performs a search for the kinds of products or services you offer.

To benefit from local citations, it's essential that you set up a Google My Business profile, claim your business, and optimize it by adding your business name and details to directories and other websites.

What Kinds of Citations Are There?

Types of citations include:
- Business directories (Yellow Pages, Yelp, etc.)
- Industry, niche, or sector-specific directories (Trip Advisor)
- Local newspaper and press websites
- Local themed blogs
- Prominent local websites (primarily when related to your business niche)
- Social Profiles (Twitter, Instagram, Facebook, etc.)

How Can I Use Citations to Beat My Competition?

The short answer is that you need more high-quality citations than your competitors. Although the total number of citations is important, the quality of the directory where your citation is listed is also very important, and so is the accuracy of the information that you enter.

If you want your Google Map citations to rank high on Google Local listings, then you need to make sure that your general and niche citations are complete because this will create value and improve your visibility and presence within all of Google maps products.

It's easier to obtain a business listing citation, but it's a little trickier to obtain a local or niche website citation. You'll need to have something newsworthy for these local websites and newspapers to talk about, and you'll have to get their attention in order for them to want to write about you. If you have anything newsworthy to report, we recommend releasing a digital press release on your website to announce the news.

How Can I Make an Excellent Local Citation?

For a great local citation, both individual people and Google itself need to see your business as credible and trustworthy. To help build trust and credibility, always include three pieces of critical information when creating or claiming your business directory style citation:

1. Your business name
2. Your local telephone number including your local area code
3. Your business' physical address

This information is vital when creating and filling out both the general and industry-specific directories.

It's important that these three pieces of information are both present and consistent on your website as selectable HTML text and not as a graphic.

What Should I Keep in Mind?

If your business is in a particular niche or obscure area that you are unable to describe using a broad or general category, then it might not be a good idea to invest in a Local SEO campaign to appear in the Google Map Pack.17

Local SEO only helps improve your rankings where your listing appears within the Google Maps Pack, which is sometimes referred to as the seven pack since this is the number of results Google will usually display.

---

17 https://thrivehive.com/rank-higher-google-maps/

Google Maps specifically focuses on keywords as they pertain to location; these keywords heavily favor local businesses or services. For instance, Restaurants, Gyms, Garages, and Grocery Stores are good examples of local companies.

Keep in mind that only specific phrases trigger the maps to show in the results. For example, if you search for "Garage," the map citations will not appear, but if you search for "Garage Near Me," then the map citations will be displayed. When it comes to Voice Search, the Voice Assistant will default to the "near me" option.

Step 4

Update Your 'Google My Business' Profile

One of the most important things you can do for your Voice Rankings is to fully update Google My Business, the Google platform through which local businesses are linked to their environment. We'll be looking at this in more detail in the next section.

When someone searches for businesses and places near their location, they are shown numerous places across Google Maps and Google Search. You want your business to show up on this list!

Searching for 'Doughnut Shops'.

Figure 7: 'Google My Business'

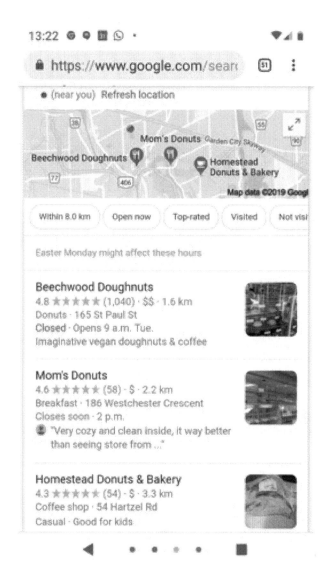

As you can see from the picture above, if you search for "doughnut shops" from your mobile device it would look something like this. Google aims to show you the kind of nearby shops you'd like to visit. So, if you happen to own a doughnut shop and you have a Google Business Profile it will appear in the results. This makes it easier for your business to stand out and attract new customers. And it's especially important for Voice Search because this is the list that your Voice Assistant will read to potential customers.

How to Claim and Update your 'Google My Business'.

A. Ensure All Business Information Is Entered Correctly

Google's local results give preference to the most relevant results for each search query. It's easier for Google to match your business with the appropriate search query if all of your business' information is complete and accurate. Once all of your business' information has been entered in Google My Business, customers will know more about what you do, where you are located, and when they can visit you.

Important information includes (but is not limited to) your physical address, phone number, category, and attributes. Make sure this information is updated as your business changes.

Here are the steps you need to follow to add or claim your Business Profile:

1. Open Google My Business.
2. At the top right of the page click Sign in
3. Sign in to your Google Account, or create a new one.
4. Type in the name of your business, and click Next.
5. Type in the location of your business and click Next.
6. Select if you'd like your business location to appear on Google Maps.

   6a. If you serve customers at your business address:

   -Type in your business address and click Next.

   Note: If you serve customers outside your business address, there is an option to list your other service areas.

   6b. If you don't serve customers at your business address:

   -Enter your business address.

   -At the bottom, click I deliver goods and services to my customers and click Next.

   -List your service areas, then click Next.

7. Select a business category from the search field and click Next.
8. Type in your business' phone number or website URL and click Next. Note: there is also the option to create a free website based on your information.
9. To complete the sign-up and verify your connection to this business, click Finish.
10. Choose a verification option.

-To verify at a later time, click More options → Later. You must be authorized to manage the business, otherwise find the person in charge and continue.

If you see a message that says, "This listing has already been claimed," click request access and follow the directions to claim your business. You can Learn more about how to do that here.

B. Verify Your Business Listing

Once your business listing has been created, you must verify it in order to manage your business information in Search, Maps, and other Google properties. The verification process helps Google ensure that your business information is accurate and that only you, the business owner or manager, has access to it. Learn more about verification

Once your business is verified with Google, it will appear on Google Search and Google Maps. Most local companies opt to verify their business by mail. However, other verification options include email, phone, or Search Console.

C. Make Sure Your Business Hours are Accurate

By keeping your opening hours up to date and including special hours for holidays and events, potential customers will know when you are available, and it will help build trust in your company, which Google takes into consideration.

Follow these steps to set your hours:

- Sign in to Google My Business. If you have multiple locations, open the location you'd like to manage.
- Click Info on the menu.
- Click "Add hours."
- Select each day of the week that your business is open and set it to "on".
- For each day of the week that your business is open, click Opens At, and then choose the opening time.
- Next to each day of the week that your business is open, click Closes At, and then choose the closing time.
- Once you're finished setting your hours, click Apply.

D. Interact with Your Customers by Responding to Reviews

When a customer leaves a review, it's a good idea to interact with them. When you respond to reviews, it shows that you care about your customers and the feedback they are giving you. Positive reviews work wonders for improving your business' visibility and increasing the chances that potential customers will buy from you.

> *Tip*
> *Create a link that customers can easily click on to write reviews and encourage them to give you feedback.*

How to Create a Customer Review Link

Follow these steps to create a link using Google Search:
- Search for your business on Google using your computer.
- Find your business listing and click on "write a review."
- Copy and paste the URL you see in your address bar.

If these steps don't work for you, use the PlaceID Lookup Tool instead:

Type in your business name in the "Enter a location" field at the top of the map.
- Click on your business name from the list that appears.
- Copy your Place ID, which you'll see underneath your business name.
- Add your Place ID to the following URL to create your link:
  https://search.google.com/local/writereview?placeid=<place_id>

E. Add Photos

Adding photos is a great way to tell your business' story. It also shows your customers and potential customers your goods and services, making them more willing to buy. And again, it builds trust with Google too.

To add photos, follow these steps:
1. Sign in to Google My Business. If you have multiple locations, open the location you'd like to manage.
2. From the menu, click Photos.
3. Select the kind of photo or video you'd like to add.
4. Upload the photo or video from your computer, or select one you've already uploaded.

F. Be in Control of How Customers See Your Business

Google bases local results primarily on relevance, distance, and prominence. Google combines these factors to help find the best match for a search. For instance, Google algorithms might decide that a business that's further from your location is more likely to be relevant to your needs than a closer business, so they will rank it higher in local results.

That's why it's essential that you leverage the power of Google My Business by keeping all your information accurate and up to date. When you use Google My Business, you're in control of what your customers and potential customers are seeing when they enter relevant search queries. This is a real boost to your SEO.

Step 5

Optimize for Local Searches

Local content is particularly popular with Voice Search and you can use this to your advantage. Here's an interesting fact: A report by Internet Trends found that 22% of people[18] use Voice Search to find local information including business hours, nearby restaurants, or even just "things to do near me". Google even stated[19] that "near me" searches have grown by over 146% year after year.

And the best part? 50% of local mobile searches [20]by a consumer resulted in a visit to the store that same day.

If you're asking yourself, how can I use voice search to gain more business? The answer is to incorporate the following keywords into your SEO strategy carefully:

- -The phrases people use to describe the area where your business is located.

- -Use "Near me" in your title tags, meta description, internal links, and anchor text.

- -Talk about landmarks close by to your business.

- -Use the titles of local institutions that are relevant to your business.

- -Include the hours your business is open.

- -Attach a photo of your store to your Google Business Account.

- -Include a Google Map on your website so customers can find you.

---

18 Neil Patel https://neilpatel.com/blog/seo-for-voice-search/

19 Lisa Gebelber https://www.thinkwithgoogle.com/consumer-insights/build-your-mobile-centric-search-strategy/

20 Jessica Lee https://searchenginewatch.com/sew/study/2343577/google-local-searches-lead-50-of-mobile-users-to-visit-stores-study

- -Always keep in mind the classic 5 W's: Who, What, Where, When, Why, and (bonus) How because conversational searches ask these questions.

Figure 8: Question Phrases by Voice Search

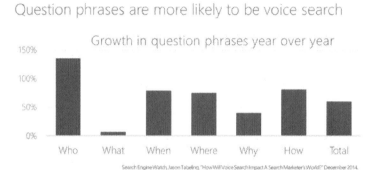

Question phrases are more likely to be voice search

Growth in question phrases year over year

Search Engine Watch, Jason Tabeling, "How Will Voice Search Impact A Search Marketer's World?" December 2014.

Step 6

Search Result Snippet & Meta Tags

Whenever someone enters a search in Google, your meta description, title, and slug will appear in Google's result page listing. It works the same way in Voice Search, except this is what Alexa, Siri, or Google will tell you about the business based on what they "see" in the listing. It looks like this:

Figure 9: Snippet

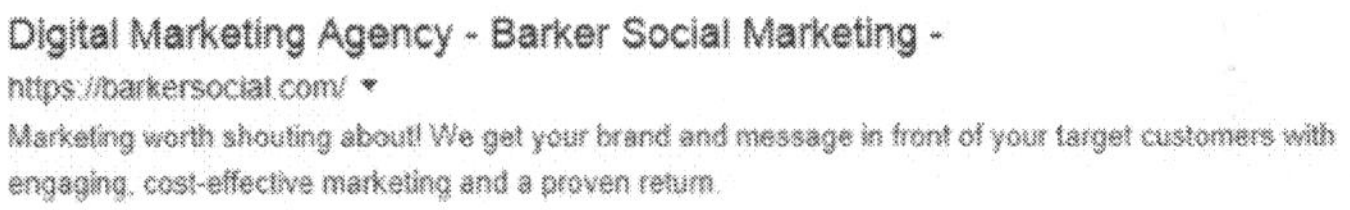

Digital Marketing Agency - Barker Social Marketing -
https://barkersocial.com/ ▾
Marketing worth shouting about! We get your brand and message in front of your target customers with engaging, cost-effective marketing and a proven return.

Meta descriptions, which are sometimes called search descriptions, are short pieces of copy that sum up your website's content. Meta descriptions are shown underneath the page title in search results.

For example, in the screenshot above the meta description says:
> "Marketing worth shouting about! We get your brand and message in front of your target customers with engaging, cost-effective marketing and a proven return."

The title is: "Digital Marketing Agency - Barker Social Marketing"

The slug is: https://barkersocial.com/

How Metadata Descriptions Boost SEO

Although your search rankings won't be directly affected by your metadata information, it will affect your click-through-rate, and the click-through-rate improves your SEO. (Even if you're not physically clicking with Voice Search, it still counts towards the click-through-rate.) When you use the snippet editor on your website builder (ex: WordPress or Squarespace) to modify your posts' description, you have the chance to write copy that will grab your reader's attention, which in turn, improves your click-through-rate. The more clicks you receive, the higher your website will rank on Google.

Google's algorithms determine what appears on a page for any given search query, or what is read aloud in a voice query. It's impossible to keep descriptions exactly the same for every potential search but making sure these descriptions are filled will impact how your site ranks in search engines. If for some reason the wrong information is displaying in search results you can request a re-index using Google Search Console.

How to Write Proper Metadata Descriptions

You always want to put yourself in your visitor's shoes: What is your ideal audience searching for? When you're writing your metadata think about what your business does. What problems are you solving for your target market? How can you convince them that your website is what they are looking for and encourage them to click through?

The answers to these questions should be included in your metadata.

Best practices for metadata include:

- Using keywords to optimize your descriptions while avoiding keyword stuffing
- Making sure the text stays between 50-300 characters
- Ensuring your descriptions are short, relevant, and easily readable

How to Update Your Metadata

All metadata can be updated through your website builder such as WordPress or Squarespace. Each time you create a new post you can modify the meta description, title, and slug so that it's easily readable and gives your reader a nice taste of what your post is about—prompting them to click on it and boosting your SEO.

Step 7

Security Matters – SSL

Another easy but important step is to ensure you have a Secure SSL Certificate (https:) for your website. This will impact both your regular website SEO and also your Voice Search results.

If your website doesn't have an SSL certificate, Google displays a 'Not Secure' sign in the URL bar. It's the difference between HTTP and HTTPS and that difference makes a serious impact.

Figure 10: SSL Warning

Of course, you want your customers and potential customers to feel safe when browsing your website. You do not want to be penalized in the search rankings for missing the "s".

Here's everything you need to know about adding an SSL certificate to your site.

What is an SSL Certificate?

SSL stands for Secure Sockets Layer. It's the standard security technology that establishes an encrypted link between a web server and a browser. This encrypted link makes sure that all data passed between the web server and browsers stays private and integral.

Without an SSL certificate, no secure connection can be established. That means, your business' information will not be connected digitally to a cryptographic key.

An SSL Certificate contains the following information:
- The holder's name
- The serial number and expiration date
- A copy of your public key
- A digital signature of the certificate-issuing authority

Why are SSL Certificates Important?

Do you want random computers to see your credit card numbers, usernames, passwords, and other sensitive data? Unless you've got a screw loose, the answer should be NO. And neither do your customers.

But all the information you send over the internet is passed from computer to computer until it arrives at its destination server. That means if your information is not encrypted then any computer in between you and the server can see all your private data.

That's why SSL certificates are so important. An SSL certificate ensures that all of that sensitive information remains encrypted, so even when it's passed from computer to computer, it can't be read. When an SSL certificate is used, your private data becomes unreadable to everyone except for the server you're sending the information to.

Many hacks are transit-based, meaning your information is stolen as it moves from computer to computer on its way to the destination server. An SSL certificate provides a necessary means of protecting you against these transit-based hacks.

You need an SSL for your SEO

Not only does not having HTTPS diminish customer trust but it also negatively impacts your Google rankings.

Having an SSL certificate boosts your SEO because Google values security. When a site is trusted more, people will visit it. Plus, Google is already beginning to favor HTTPS sites over HTTP, and this will only increase as time goes on.

Since 2014, Google has implemented algorithms that favor HTTPS websites and penalize websites missing the SSL certificate. These algorithms have tightened and become stronger and stronger. Now in 2019, having an SSL is critical if you want to be listed anywhere near page 1 of Google's listings.

Never forget that better Google rankings result in better traffic to your website. Not only will an SSL indicate to potential customers that they can trust you, it will ensure they can find you on Google.

An HTTPS site also loads much faster than HTTP, which is another boost to your SEO and your brand power.

How Does an SSL Certificate Build Brand Power?

When your website has an SSL certificate, your customers and potential customers, see a lock icon next to the URL and a green address bar. This shows your customers that an SSL certificate is in use, encrypting all their sensitive data.

Figure 11: SSL Secure

When your customers see this, they know they can trust your business and that builds brand power.

How Do I Install an SSL Certificate?

Setting up an SSL certificate on your website is easy. There are three simple steps to follow:

1. If you have a website, then you have a hosting company supporting that website. If you don't have a plan with a dedicated IP address ask your current web host company to upgrade your account, so it has a dedicated IP address.
2. Next, you need to buy an SSL certificate which you can do from your host or companies like ssls.com, NameCheap, ssl2buy.com, etc.
3. Once you've purchased an SSL certificate ask your web hosting company to activate it and install it for you. Once this is done if you go to https://yoursite.com, you should see it load and your website will be secure.

Figure 12: SSL Secure Icon

Google will favor you so much more when you've completed this step, which will help your Voice Search rankings.

Part 3:

Next Steps

- Tying It All Together
- Getting Help & Hiring an Expert
- About Us
- Comments & Questions

Tying it All Together

Voice Search is clearly becoming an essential part of any great SEO strategy. Its growth and popularity are not slowing down in the least and disruption in the field of online search is very real. This is bad for businesses who ignore the trend and create the same old content. Don't be like the photo industry that ignored the changing preferences of consumer demand for digital pictures, or the music industry's ignorance of digital music; get ahead of the curve and don't wait until it's too late.

Voice Search will be an incredible tool for early adopting businesses who update their digital strategies now, not later. If you start optimizing your content for Voice Search, ensuring that your content is closer to human language and providing answers to custom questions, you will get a leg up on the competition! And now is the perfect time to jump on the Voice Search SEO bandwagon.

Getting Help & Hiring an Expert

If you've been completing the 7 steps as you went through this book, then you're on the right track. Just remember to revisit your online materials on a regular basis, monthly. Of if you're keeping a blog, then weekly or even several times a week can contribute to higher rankings.

If, however, you've now read through the entire book and are feeling a bit overwhelmed, or simply don't have the time to do all the things, than you should make a plan to tackle the steps in a practical manner, like by tackling 1-2 two steps a week. Gather your team and work together as a group, have a brainstorming session, and begin tackling the steps one at a time.

If you still feel you need help getting this important work completed so that you can rank by Voice Search, you can hire a professional and have them do it for you. If you're looking for help you can reach us at our website or by email.

barkersocial.com
barker@barkersocial.com

About The Authors

Jessica Zeitz
@jesszeitz

A natural born writer, Jessica started journaling from the age of seven, following her passion in school with a diploma in English literature and a bachelor's degree in Communications. After graduation, she spent a year traveling South-East Asia and discovered the world of remote work, where she was able to combine her love of travel and writing by freelancing. A multi-tasking machine Jess puts both her English and French skills to work through professional copywriting and translation for any industry. She thrives in fast-paced environments and loves to take on any project Barker Social throws at her.
When she isn't writing or dreaming up her next destination, Jess enjoys pickling and poetry.

Mandi Gould
@barker_social

Mandi knows how to get things done. She has a tremendous drive for planning and an unstoppable ability to churn out quality marketing content. Her creative spirit, project management skills, and copywriting ability make her a marketing dynamo. She's been an entrepreneur since 1999 and her portfolio ranges from work in the arts, to food and beverage, health and wellness, four years in the corporate world, and much more. Before Barker Social, she successfully launched, operated, and sold two businesses and she thrives on writing compelling marketing copy for international businesses of all sizes.
Where there's a quality idea and work worth doing, Mandi will realize the project. She's also a bird lover, health foodie, jazz enthusiast, and swing dancer.

Allan Munro
@DAllanMunro

Allan is a big picture thinker and is able to creatively connect the dots. With over 25 years of experience as a sales and marketing professional with Kodak and ADP and E-commerce startups, Allan is able to bring together rigorous analysis and sales planning, big data analysis, creative thinking, process optimization, and strategic planning to the projects he's engaged on.

If Allan isn't building a house in his spare time or making a piece of heirloom furniture, Allan is a dedicated father of two young boys who are the best part of his days (except the 5am wakeups).

Comments Questions & Suggestions

If you have any comments, questions or feedback we're happy to hear from you. Please send us an email to: **datalore@dateloreanalytics.com**

Appendix

Works Cited

"How to Optimize for Voice Search: 4 Simple SEO Strategies." Neil Patel, Neil Patel, 15 July 2018, neilpatel.com/blog/seo-for-voice-search/.

"How to Prepare for Voice Search • Yoast." Yoast, 6 Nov. 2017, yoast.com/voice-search/.

Manufactured by Amazon.ca
Bolton, ON